MAKING FRIENDS IN MALI

by Caroline Harris
illustrated by Donna Perrone

PEARSON

Scott
Foresman

Editorial Offices: Glenview, Illinois • Parsippany, New Jersey • New York, New York
Sales Offices: Needham, Massachusetts • Duluth, Georgia • Glenview, Illinois
Coppell, Texas • Ontario, California • Mesa, Arizona

CHAPTER 1 THE DECISION

"What's Goumbou?" asked Charlie Zeroulias. He had heard his mother saying the word as he banged through the screen door into the kitchen.

"It's a town in Mali, a country in western Africa," replied his mother, without looking up from the atlas she and his father were studying intently.

Charlie had just gotten out of school, and he was hot and hungry. "Goumbou" sounded like gumbo to him, a spicy stew his mother cooked occasionally. He wasn't crazy about it.

He glanced over at his parents. His mother, Helena, had a worried look on her face. Wrinkles stretched across her brow. His father, Costas, was bent over the old atlas, estimating distances with his thumb. From the tip of the thumb to the first joint measures about an inch. In this case, an inch on the atlas maps equaled 134 miles.

"If you go in a straight line, it's more than one hundred miles from the capital," said Costas.

"What is? What are you talking about?" asked Charlie as he poked his head in the fridge and started rummaging for food.

"Goumbou," replied his mother. "Georgia will be moving there soon. She has decided to join the Peace Corps as a volunteer."

Charlie yanked his head out of the fridge and stared at his parents for a moment. "Georgia?" he asked, forgetting that he had been faint with hunger just a minute before.

Georgia was his favorite sister and the oldest child in the family. Charlie, at eleven, was the youngest. The two were good friends; at least they were when Georgia was home.

For the past four years Georgia had been at college. But she had written Charlie frequently while away. Charlie loved receiving Georgia's letters and had kept every one of them. He could always recite to his parents what Georgia's favorite classes were or the worst dining hall food she had eaten.

Of course, what Charlie preferred most of all was when his sister came home! But Georgia only returned home for vacations and the summer. This summer, Charlie hoped, she would come home for good. He needed her help with all kinds of projects. He wanted to build a new raft for the river, or make the one they built last year sturdy enough for two people. He wanted to finish the fort they had started in the woods some time ago. No one else ever seemed to have time to help him with any of these things. But Georgia did, and now she was going to Africa? *Africa is so far away,* Charlie thought to himself. *Why would Georgia want to move there?*

Charlie had learned a little bit about the Peace Corps in school. It was an organization that sent Americans around the world to help people in other countries. *Why couldn't Georgia just stay home and help out right here?* Charlie grumbled to himself.

The Zeroulias family ran a garden center. Customers came from all over to buy their colorful flowers. The family had hoped Georgia would join the business after graduation since she was the first one in her family to go to college. They needed her experience to continue to improve the business. The garden center had been a tumbledown place when Costas and Helena bought it. Old pictures showed a sagging greenhouse and a barn with a huge hole in the roof. Who could run a business there? people wondered. "The Zerouliases could," announced Costas proudly whenever anyone asked.

With his own hands Costas had repaired the greenhouse and even built a small apartment over the barn for his family to live in. Twenty-two years later, it was still their home, though it had grown crowded as more Zeroulias kids were born. Georgia shared a room with her two younger sisters, Anastasia and Etta. They slept in a triple-decker bed built by their father. Charlie had his bed in the hall, but it folded into the wall during the day. While Costas had done all the building, Helena had been busy making the apartment into a home for the family. She had sewn beautiful bedspreads for everyone and hung up colorful curtains in all the rooms. Georgia, Charlie, and their sisters learned that helping out was a way of life. Making a home out of a barn was an efficient and simple way to live. That's how Costas Zeroulias liked things to be.

Other than simplicity and efficiency, there was one other thing that Costas prized: ambition. He had a desire to improve things. He was dedicated to watering and weeding his flowers, so they would be healthy and beautiful. The great care he took led to the success of his business. Costas was proud when he heard customers claim his flowers were the most beautiful ones they had ever seen.

"Don't you want to do your best?" he used to ask if his children did a sloppy job on their homework or rushed through helping with a chore in the greenhouse. "Where's your ambition?"

Georgia had known he would ask that same question when she called to announce her decision to join the Peace Corps. They had worked hard to make sure she got the education they never had. Her classmates would all be starting careers and earning money. She was going to give up opportunities like that to become a volunteer? Where was her ambition? Knowing that her father would question her decision, Georgia had already prepared an answer.

"I'm just like you, Dad," Georgia explained to her father. "I want to improve things, but I want to do it in a place that needs it more than here. So many people have helped me, and now it's my turn to be the helper." Costas was silent for a moment. "I want to be a teacher," Georgia added. "But how can I teach unless I know about the world?"

She was right. Costas realized that now as he studied the map of West Africa, tracing the blue line of the Niger River as it wound its way through Mali. *Georgia was right about all of it.* That knowledge buoyed his spirits and he found himself suddenly proud that his daughter had found her own path to follow.

"Georgia will be just fine," Costas said to Helena. "There's nothing for us to worry about."

Helena smiled. She was thinking about the track meet Georgia had competed in the week before. It was the final race of the season, and Georgia had given it her best effort. She had come in second place—not bad for a girl who had never run track until last year. But that's the way it was with Georgia, once she decided to do something, nothing could stop her.

"Watch out, Mali," said Helena. "Here comes Georgia!"

"Goumbou," said Charlie, wandering out of the kitchen and rolling the new word around on his tongue. "Goumbou."

CHAPTER 2 GETTING READY

In just one week Georgia would be leaving her family and traveling to Mali. It was totally different from the coast of Maine, where Georgia's family lived. Mali was a hot, flat, and landlocked country.

Thinking about Maine made Georgia's mind wander. She thought back to the springtimes of her youth. Spring in Maine was cool, wet, and bursting with green. Each year she and Charlie had a contest to see who could spy the first shoots pushing up in the garden and woods. Charlie usually won.

"You notice everything," Georgia always said in amazement. Charlie did notice everything; that's how he found most of the treasures he collected. One of them was a flat stone about the size of a quarter he found on the beach one day.

"Look at that. It's shaped like a heart," Georgia said. "You should save it." Charlie dropped it in his pocket. He was fascinated by its shape. The stone had been tossed by the waves and ground by the sand, yet somehow it had formed a perfect heart.

That day Charlie also found a piece of rock washed up on the beach that was filled with holes and looked just like a golf ball. Charlie had no idea what it was, so he handed it to Georgia to inspect.

"It's pumice," she announced, after examining it. "It's a type of volcanic glass. Again, great find, Charlie," she exclaimed. Charlie put the pumice in his pocket with the heart stone. He was sure it would come in handy for something.

"Charlie?" Georgia called to him from her room one day as she was getting ready for her trip to Africa. She was sitting on the bottom bunk reading letters from other Peace Corps volunteers. Next to her was a heaping pile of things she had been gathering to take, including clothes and batteries. But she was missing something important, or so one letter said.

Charlie poked his head around the corner. He wanted to help.

"Remember last year when we went to the beach? And you found some pumice? Guess what? I just learned it would be helpful to have in Mali," said Georgia. "Would you let me take it along?"

"For what?" asked Charlie.

"For my feet," explained Georgia. "This letter says I'll need to use it to sand my heels to keep them from cracking in the dry heat."

"Sure, if I can find it." said Charlie. "Dry heat, huh? Maybe we could bring some of that to Maine!" Charlie added. Then he disappeared into the hall.

Georgia turned back to her letters and read a little more. They were filled with advice from other volunteers who had been to Mali. "Don't bother with sneakers and socks," wrote one volunteer. "It's too hot. Wear sandals. The sun is strong. You'll need a hat. For fun, bring a Frisbee. And don't forget to bring stamps—plenty of them. You will be writing home a lot."

Georgia looked up. How many stamps would she use in twenty-seven months? That was how long she would be in Mali. She thought about all the letters she had written while away at college—Charlie had stacks of them. Sometimes they reread them together when she was home. Together they had laughed about the silly food she had eaten and imitated her ridiculous professors.

Suddenly twenty-seven months seemed like a huge amount of time to be gone. Georgia thought of all the things that would happen at home while she was gone and how much would change. Her parents would probably build the new greenhouse they had been planning. And her dad was talking about growing some new varieties of flowers. Her mom had plans to make tablecloths for the kitchen and pillows for the living room. Anastasia would go off to college, while Etta would get her driver's license. And Charlie? Would she even recognize him when she came back? He would be a teenager. His voice would be deep and he might tower over her.

Georgia realized it would be hard to be away for so long. She knew her family would write to her, but Mali was far away and it might take a long time for their letters to reach her. She wondered if any of the volunteers had any advice about missing home and family.

The next letter Georgia looked at told her to bring photos from home. "It will make you happy to have them posted on the walls of your hut," the letter said. "The villagers will be curious to see pictures of your family and home too," it added.

Georgia had bought a small, sturdy camera for the trip and several rolls of film. She had used one roll right away to take pictures of things she knew she would miss. These would be her memories for two long years. She glanced through the pictures for a moment before packing them away.

She had taken pictures of everything. Her favorite trees in the yard looked lush and green in the photos. From what she had read about Mali's dry landscape, she imagined things would look very different there. The raft she and Charlie had built looked as if it still needed a little work. Georgia smiled, though, thinking about the fun they'd had building it. She stared at the picture of her bedroom that showed Anastasia and Etta sitting on their bunks, making silly faces with flashlights.

There were endless pictures showing Charlie. *How did he get in so many pictures?* Georgia wondered. Georgia had taken one of her mother and father standing just inside the greenhouse, with all their different-colored flowers in bloom behind them. Popping up between the tables of plants was Charlie, grinning from ear to ear. Georgia couldn't help but smile, seeing how silly he looked in the photo.

Georgia had even photographed the henhouse that her father had built out of wood, complete with a pointed roof. She remembered the day the two of them had spent painting it. Costas liked to joke that it was a finer house than the family lived in. The chickens had clucked loudly the day it was finished, so Georgia was confident they liked it too.

The Zerouliases were one of the few families around that still kept chickens. They sold the eggs to make a little extra money each week. It was another way Costas felt his family could live more efficiently. Helena always cooked a big breakfast with the eggs that hadn't been sold. It was a favorite meal of everyone in the family, since Helena would cook the eggs any way Costas and the children wanted them done. Georgia was always amazed at how her mother could keep their requests straight.

Looking at the photograph of the henhouse made Georgia think about the chickens they kept. Her favorite was a Rhode Island Red hen. It was big and handsome and laid more eggs than any other hen in the henhouse. Her brother's favorite was one of the older and plumper roosters. Georgia laughed to herself, thinking of how much her brother Charlie loved that chicken, despite how loud it was. After being woken up by one of its early-morning crows, Charlie would always say, "How could one little bird make so much noise?" Of course, Georgia had pictures of both the hen and the rooster.

Now, sitting on her bed, Georgia looked at the last photo in the collection. It was a picture of Charlie holding the rooster while trying to crow as loudly as the bird. Charlie's head was tilted, and his mouth was open. Georgia could almost hear the combined noise of Charlie and the bird squawking.

Just then there was a loud thud in the hall. In bounded Charlie with his hands behind his back.

"I have something for you," he said. "Guess which hand it's in." She had played this game with Charlie countless times before, but she never guessed right. Or if by some miracle she *did* guess right, he would trick her by switching the surprise to his other hand. This time she wanted to win!

"Both hands," said Georgia.

"You're right," shouted Charlie, sticking both hands out.

In one hand was the pumice, and the other held the heart-shaped stone. Georgia caught her breath at the sight of the flat, little stone. Charlie had admired it so much, and now he was giving it to her. She studied Charlie for a moment so she'd have a mental image of him to take on her upcoming trip. He was very thin—like a parking meter, she thought. His hands were broad, and always dirty. His hair was fine and shaggy. In the mornings, parts of it stuck up, just like springtime shoots in the garden.

"Oh, Charlie," said Georgia. She dropped her photos on the bed and gave him a big hug.

CHAPTER 3 GEORGIA ARRIVES IN MALI

It wasn't until the airplane bounced down the runway and came to a stop that Georgia realized just how far she had traveled. She was now in Africa! She gazed out the window at the flat land dotted with small bushes and a few trees. She could see the heat rising off the runway in shimmering waves. The sun was beating down hard. It seemed to her that it had bleached all the color from the land.

Tired as she was, Georgia was tingling with excitement. This was the start of her great adventure! She would spend the first three months learning French and Bambara, the two main languages spoken in Mali. Georgia already spoke French quite well. She had started studying it in fifth grade and continued all the way through college. But with Bambara she would have to start from the beginning. She wasn't really worried, though.

"Bambara is probably one of the easiest African languages to learn," another volunteer had told her.

There would be a lot to learn in those three months besides the Bambaran language. Her training would also include lessons in farming, since Georgia's job in Mali would be to help farmers find ways to improve their crops. She would also help them raise more chickens. Georgia already felt comfortable with those tasks. Wasn't her Rhode Island Red the best egg layer in the henhouse? And the Zerouliases' vegetable garden was envied around the neighborhood.

Thinking about her family's vegetable garden made Georgia remember her childhood. She recalled the hot summer afternoons she spent with her brother and sisters weeding the garden. She remembered how enjoyable it was to nibble on different vegetables as they worked through the rows. Charlie was the speediest of all at weeding. Georgia wasn't quite sure how he did it so fast. She wished she had studied his weeding method before coming to Mali. Maybe it would have given her something useful to share with the people here.

With all she had to do, twenty-seven months in Mali hardly seemed like enough time at all! She couldn't wait to get started. Pulling her sun hat low over her brow, Georgia stepped off the plane into the rippling heat waves.

CHAPTER 4 MALI DAYS AND NIGHTS

Georgia sat bolt upright in bed, her mosquito netting tangled around her. What was that noise? It had startled her out of a sweaty sleep. There it was again, a wheezy and sharp bellowing sound. Awake now, she finally recognized the sound of a donkey braying. What a racket! It was one of many sounds she had been trying to get used to since her arrival. There was a lot to get used to here. Georgia hadn't realized just how hard it would be to settle into a new place and a new life. Sometimes she felt like crying. She had never been one to do that before.

Her new home was a two-room mud hut with a metal roof in a small village near Goumbou. It had neither electricity nor running water. She used a kerosene lantern for light at night and pulled her water from a well in the courtyard. A tall wall surrounded the courtyard, so to get in and out, Georgia had to pass through a metal door.

The first thing she did when she moved in was post the photos of her family on the walls around the hut. She stuck the one of Charlie crowing with the rooster right next to her bed. *Talk about awful noises!* Georgia thought to herself. That picture still made her laugh, and it made the villagers laugh too. She had passed it around when they came to greet her, and it had helped to start conversations. Georgia's Bambara was still rough, and conversations were not yet easy.

Speaking Bambara all day was exhausting. So was the heat. With its tin roof, Georgia's hut felt like an oven. The sun was scorching, and some days the temperature rose to 115 degrees. At night she dreamed about swimming in the cold waters off Maine. It was always the same dream, the one in which she would plunge in and feel the icy water wash over her from head to toe. She would swim until she was stiff with cold . . . and then wake up, sticky from the heat. Georgia didn't think she would ever adjust.

The heat wasn't the worst of her troubles. Georgia was a get-up-and-go person and liked to get things done. Growing up, she had made to-do lists for herself and checked off each task as she finished it. Somehow, in Mali, she didn't seem to be good at that anymore because something always got in the way. Lately it was the weather. During the rainy season, violent storms rumbled through her village several times a week. First came the sand, whipped up from the dry ground by the wind, which made everyone run for cover. Then came the thunder, crashing around Georgia's hut. Rain turned the roads to mud. If she had planned to visit a nearby farmer on her bike, the rain would force her to give up and stay home. Her ideas for planting soybeans and building better chicken coops would have to wait. But waiting made her feel useless. Would she ever be able to do all the things she had dreamed of doing?

One day, shut inside as the rain beat against her hut, Georgia heard a thumping on her door. Who would be out in this weather? She was used to people dropping by, but never during a storm. She opened the door and a short, thin man tumbled in. He was soaked and shivering, but somehow he managed to smile. It was a big, warm smile that made Georgia like him right away, and they hadn't even said a word to each other!

The man introduced himself as Moussa. He lived far from Goumbou, he said, in a tiny village twenty-five kilometers away. He had borrowed a moped to make the trip since it was too far to travel by bike over the dirt roads. He had heard about Georgia and her farming projects. What he wanted to know was, could she help him?

Georgia was impressed. Most of the people she worked with in Mali lived nearby; it was easy for them to seek her out. Moussa must really need her help if he had come so far. *Ambition* was the word that came to her mind for describing Moussa. The word made her think of her father.

Moussa asked, could she come back with him now so they could get started on his projects right away? The weather was clearing, and she could ride on the back of the moped. Moussa promised that he'd bring her back at the end of the day.

How could she say no? Moussa and his plans were just what she had been waiting for! Georgia grabbed her knapsack, slung it on her back, and followed Moussa out to the moped. Off they rolled, splashing through the puddles.

CHAPTER 5 MOUSSA AND IBRAHIM

When the moped bounced into Moussa's village, the children nearby stopped what they were doing and stared. Georgia was sitting straight and tall on the back. Who—or what—had Moussa brought with him? The youngest children rushed to find their mothers and hide behind their skirts. Georgia knew she looked strange to them, but reassured herself that things were always that way when an outsider came to a new place. "Toubab," the children would call, running after her once they had gotten over their surprise. It meant "foreigner," and reminded Georgia of how far she had to go before she could truly call Mali her home.

Moussa pulled up in front of his hut in the late afternoon. The comforting sound of someone pounding millet filled the air. It was Moussa's wife, Aminata. With her were their four children, who Moussa introduced to Georgia. Ibrahim, the oldest, had a big, warm smile just like his father's. There was something about Ibrahim that seemed so familiar to Georgia. What was it?

Her thoughts were interrupted by Moussa whisking her off to show her everything. He took her to the shelter where he kept his ducks and chickens. He showed Georgia his fields. He climbed to the roof of his hut and pointed out where he dried his vegetables so his family would have food after the growing season. Ibrahim followed everywhere.

Moussa had big plans, and Georgia was immediately impressed with his ambition. It made her think of her father and how he had transformed an old battered barn and greenhouse into their home, as well as a thriving business.

Moussa wanted to raise more chickens, but he needed a larger house for them. He had all sorts of questions for Georgia on the matter. Moussa wanted to know, could she recommend a way to build a better one? What could she tell him about planting soybeans? Would the plants grow in his soil, and where should he plant them? Thinking about her family's garden, Georgia was certain she could help Moussa. She was impressed to hear that he had already heard of using a solar dryer for vegetables. Moussa peppered her with questions on that subject also. Did she know how to make one? he asked. How long would it take?

Ibrahim listened to his father's questions, and Georgia noticed he paid close attention to every detail. Then it struck her: Ibrahim was just like Charlie! Like Charlie, he noticed everything. He was also about Charlie's height, and just as bony.

"How old are you, Ibrahim?" Georgia asked.

"Eleven," he said.

"You're the same age as my brother," Georgia said, delighted. "I'll show you a picture of him sometime."

Ibrahim grinned broadly, reminding Georgia even more of her brother.

The next time Georgia came back, she helped Moussa pick out a spot to plant a crop of soybeans. She brought a set of plans showing how to build a new chicken house. Moussa nodded with interest when she mentioned her family's bright red one. Georgia had another set of plans for the solar dryer, which would resemble a mud brick shed, with a roof made of thick, sturdy glass. The sun would pass through the glass and dry the vegetables inside.

Over the weeks, Moussa and Ibrahim worked hard on the projects. Georgia visited when she could, once riding her bike the entire way. After school Ibrahim helped to make mud bricks for the new buildings. He made so many bricks that he lost count! Still, he looked forward to Georgia's visits. Georgia was always astonished to see how much the stack of bricks had grown. She complimented Ibrahim on his progress, marveling at his ability to work quickly no matter what the weather was like. Somehow, it was easy for Georgia to speak Bambara with Ibrahim. He didn't mind her mistakes and corrected her gently when she asked for help with the language. She liked hearing stories about his village and his family. The stories helped her to understand the people of Mali and their traditions.

In return she told Ibrahim stories about her home. She described the chicken house her father had built, and her favorite hen, the Rhode Island Red. And she told him all about Charlie.

"You said you had a picture of him," Ibrahim reminded her. "Can you bring it?"

"Sure, no problem," Georgia replied.

Much of the work took place during the month of Ramadan. Ibrahim explained to Georgia that most of the people in Mali were Muslims, and Ramadan was their time of fasting. From sunrise to sunset, Ibrahim said, many Muslims neither ate nor drank during this holy month. Children of Ibrahim's age were excused from the fast. Moussa, however, was not. He was working long days without food or drink. In the hot sun of Mali, it was not easy to pass by a well and not take a gulp of water. Still, Moussa resisted the urge. Georgia again found herself impressed with Moussa's ambition. She knew Moussa and her father would get along well if they had the chance to meet. Georgia had written her family a few letters about Moussa's family and how much she liked working with them. In response she had received a letter asking how all their projects were going.

Moussa and Ibrahim finally finished the chicken coop. The soybeans that Georgia had helped them plant were already starting to sprout. And soon they would have enough bricks to complete the solar dryer! It would take only about half a day to build once they had the bricks, and Georgia planned to help.

At last, the day for building the solar dryer arrived. Moussa showed up at Georgia's door on his moped to take her to his farm, and she grabbed her picture of Charlie before they sped off. Now that the work was nearly done, Georgia sadly realized that there might be few chances left for her to visit with Moussa's family. But at least Ibrahim would now have the chance to see a picture of Charlie!

When the last brick was in place, Moussa, Ibrahim, and Georgia stepped back to admire their work. They attached the glass roof, and the dryer was finished! Now Moussa could be sure of having enough good food to feed his family. He wanted to find a way to thank Georgia. How could he show his gratitude? He thought for a minute. Suddenly, a big smile lit up his face and he disappeared into his hut. When he and Aminata returned, the two of them presented Georgia with the most beautiful piece of fabric she had ever seen.

"It's a Mali mud cloth that Aminata made," Moussa said proudly.

Georgia was touched. All she had done was share her knowledge with them, and in return they had given her something that she would treasure forever.

Georgia sighed. *What kindness I have found here*, she thought. But it was more than that. It was friendship. She looked around at the flat land and the mud huts baking in the sun. None of it seemed strange anymore. She felt the warm earth beneath her feet and heard the chickens clucking at Moussa in the chicken coop. For the first time since arriving in Mali, Georgia felt as if she belonged.

Suddenly, she remembered the picture of Charlie.

"I brought something to show you," she said to Ibrahim. She pulled the photo from her knapsack and passed it to him. Ibrahim studied it for a moment. The boy in the picture had his head cocked and his mouth was wide open. He was holding the biggest rooster Ibrahim had ever seen. Ibrahim burst out laughing.

"What's he doing?" he asked.

"He's crowing," said Georgia. "Like this." She threw her head back and crowed too, reveling in the friendship she had found.

Mali Mud Cloth

Mali is in western Africa, but a part of its culture is known around the world, thanks to a special kind of fabric. It's called mud cloth, or *bogolanfini*. As its English name suggests, mud is one of its key elements. Malians use the mud as a dye to paint striking patterns on the cloth.

Malians have made mud cloth for hundreds of years. They sew narrow strips of cotton together to form broad pieces for dyeing. The patterns on the cloth represent objects and sometimes recall important events in Mali's history. Malians pass along the meanings of these patterns from one generation to the next.

Traditionally, women in Mali wore mud cloth at important times in their lives, such as before marriage. Malians also used the cloth to make shirts or tunics for hunters. Mud cloth patterns have inspired designers in other countries. Simpler versions of these patterns can now be found on products we use every day, such as bed sheets and drinking mugs.